W9-AET-386

Pink

ABDO
Publishing Company

by **Sarah Tieck**

Big Buddy **BOOKS**
Buddy Bios

VISIT US AT
www.abdopublishing.com

Published by ABDO Publishing Company, PO Box 398166, Minneapolis, Minnesota 55439.

Copyright © 2014 by Abdo Consulting Group, Inc. International copyrights reserved in all countries. No part of this book may be reproduced in any form without written permission from the publisher. Big Buddy Books™ is a trademark and logo of ABDO Publishing Company.

Printed in the United States of America, North Mankato, Minnesota.
102013
012014

♻ PRINTED ON RECYCLED PAPER

Coordinating Series Editor: Rochelle Baltzer
Contributing Editors: Megan M. Gunderson, Marcia Zappa
Graphic Design: Maria Hosley
Cover Photograph: *AP Photo*: Todd Williamson/Invision.
Interior Photographs/Illustrations: *AP Photo*: Keystone, Walter Bieri (p. 21), Wide World Photo/Eric Jamison (p. 7),
    Britta Pedersen/picture-alliance/dpa (p. 23), Dan Steinberg (p. 27), Jordan Strauss/Invision (p. 5); *Getty Images*:
    Michael Caulfield/WireImage (p. 27), Paul Drinkwater/Network/NBCU Photo Bank via Getty Images
    (p. 10), Tabatha Fireman/Redferns (p. 15), SGranitz (pp. 9, 13), Dave Hogan (pp. 19, 21), Peter Kramer (p. 17),
    Kevin Mazur/WireImage (pp. 7, 21, 29), Kevin Winter (p. 25).

Library of Congress Cataloging-in-Publication Data

Tieck, Sarah, 1976- author.
  Pink : pop music superstar / Sarah Tieck.
    pages cm -- (Big buddy biographies)
  ISBN 978-1-62403-201-1
  1. P!nk, 1979---Juvenile literature. 2. Singers--United States--Biography--Juvenile literature. I. Title.
  ML3930.P467T54 2014
  782.42164092--dc23
  [B]
                              2013030844

Contents

Singing Star

Pink is a rock star. She has won awards for her hit albums and songs. She also writes much of her own music.

Pink became popular for her strong, independent music style. She has appeared on magazine covers. And, she has been **interviewed** on television shows.

In 2012, Pink dressed up for the American Music Awards. She performed the song "Try" during the show.

CANADA

New York

Pennsylvania

Doylestown

Ohio

West Virginia

Maryland

New Jersey

ATLANTIC OCEAN

Delaware

Virginia

Family Ties

Pink's real name is Alecia Beth Moore. She was born in Doylestown, Pennsylvania, on September 8, 1979. Her parents are Jim and Judy Moore. Her older brother is Jason.

When Alecia was young, her parents divorced. This made her feel angry. Alecia and her family went through a hard time.

Pink's parents sometimes attend events with her. They are supportive and often surprised by her work.

Starting Out

Alecia turned to music when she felt sad or angry. Around age 13, she began to **perform** in clubs in Philadelphia, Pennsylvania. She also wrote songs.

Alecia struggled with drug problems. And, she dropped out of school. People still noticed her musical talent. Around age 16, Alecia sang **pop** and **rhythm and blues** music with two different groups.

People noticed Pink's personal style as well as her music. Around 2000, she had bright pink hair!

Pink appears on television shows such as *The Tonight Show with Jay Leno* to promote her music.

First Album

The groups broke up. But, Alecia would find success as a **solo** singer. By 1998, she had stopped doing drugs. And, she **graduated** from high school. Around that time, she changed her stage name to Pink.

In 2000, Pink's first album came out. It is called *Can't Take Me Home*. It was a hit! Three of its songs were very popular. These were "Most Girls," "You Make Me Sick," and "There You Go."

New Sound

After her first album, Pink wanted to make a different kind of music. For her second album, she used more of her life story to inspire her songs.

In 2001, *Missundaztood* came out. The album sold 10 million copies! Two popular songs were "Get the Party Started" and "Don't Let Me Get Me." Pink was excited about her success and new sound.

In 2002, Pink sang "Get the Party Started" at the Kids' Choice Awards. She got slimed at the end of the song!

13

Pink has made many changes to her style over the years.

In 2003, Pink's third album came out. It is called *Try This*. This album had more of a rock sound than Pink's earlier music. It didn't sell as many copies, but it still did well.

In 2004, Pink won a **Grammy Award**. It was for Best Female Rock Vocal **Performance** for the song "Trouble." It was her second Grammy.

New Album

In 2006, Pink's fourth album came out. It is called *I'm Not Dead*. "Stupid Girls" was one of its hit songs. The album includes personal songs, such as "Who Knew." Others were about Pink's political beliefs.

Pink took extra time to work on *I'm Not Dead*. At first it was called *Long Way to Happy*.

Moving Up

In 2008, Pink's fifth album came out. It is called *Funhouse*. It includes rock songs such as "So What." The songs are about Pink's life. Many are about her troubles with her husband.

This album had several hits. It came out at number two on the Billboard 200 chart. Pink had never had an album reach so high on the charts!

Pink was excited when *Funhouse* came out! She attended parties to celebrate.

Bold and Strong

In addition to singing, Pink is an aerial (EHR-ee-uhl) dancer. Aerial dancers **perform** in the air using special ropes. Pink performs daring aerial moves during her concerts.

These moves require a strong body. So, Pink works out often. She also spends many hours learning the moves and practicing them.

Pink is sometimes high above the stage or out over the crowd. She has learned to do these moves and perform her songs at the same time!

A Singer's Life

As a singer and songwriter, Pink spends time working on her songs. She goes to recording studios to make albums.

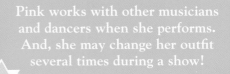

Pink works with other musicians and dancers when she performs. And, she may change her outfit several times during a show!

After an album comes out, Pink works hard to **promote** it. She appears on television and in magazines. And, she practices and plans to **perform** live for fans.

Pink often talks to fans and signs autographs.

Off the Stage

Pink spends free time with her husband, Carey Hart, and their daughter, Willow. They enjoy being active together, doing things such as snowboarding.

Pink also likes to help others. She has spoken out about protecting animals. In 2007, she **performed** in a concert called Party for Animals Worldwide (PAW).

In 2005, Pink won an award for her work with People for the Ethical Treatment of Animals (PETA).

PETA

HUMANITARIAN AWARD

presented to

P!nk

27

Buzz

Pink's sixth album is called *The Truth About Love*. It came out in 2012. One of its hit songs was "Try."

In 2013, Pink went on tour. She added some daring aerial moves to her concert **performances**. Fans are excited for more music from Pink!

29

Snapshot

★**Name**: Alecia Beth "Pink" Moore

★**Birthday**: September 8, 1979

★**Birthplace**: Doylestown, Pennsylvania

★**Albums**: *Can't Take Me Home, Missundaztood, Try This, I'm Not Dead, Funhouse, The Truth About Love*

Important Words

graduate (GRA-juh-wayt) to complete a level of schooling.

Grammy Award any of the awards given each year by the National Academy of Recording Arts and Sciences. Grammy Awards honor the year's best accomplishments in music.

interview to ask someone a series of questions.

perform to do something in front of an audience. A performance is the act of doing something, such as singing or acting, in front of an audience.

pop relating to popular music.

promote to help something become known.

rhythm and blues (RIH-thuhm) a form of popular music that features a strong beat. It is inspired by jazz, gospel, and blues styles.

solo a performance by a single person.

studio a place where music is recorded.

Web Sites

To learn more about Pink, visit ABDO Publishing Company online. Web sites about Pink are featured on our Book Links page. These links are routinely monitored and updated to provide the most current information available.

www.abdopublishing.com

Index